GEOMETRY

Math Tutor Lesson Plan Series

Book 1

iGlobal Educational Services

To order, contact iGlobal Educational Services, PO Box 94224, Phoenix, AZ 85070

Website: www.iglobaleducation.com

Fax: 512-233-5389

Geometry Book 1

Contents

Lesson 1: Triangles and Angle Relationships 6

Lesson 2: Triangle Congruence 20

Lesson 3: Trigonometric Ratios 37

Lesson 4: Applying Trigonometric Ratios 56

Introduction

Tutoring is beginning to get the respect and recognition it deserves. More and more learners require individualized or small group instruction whether it is in the classroom setting or in a private tutoring setting either face-to-face or online.

This lesson plan book is part of the series "Math Tutor Lesson Plan" Series. It is conceived and created for tutors and educators who desire to provide effective tutoring either in person or online in any educational setting, including the classroom.

Inside This Lesson Plan Book

This *Geometry: Math Tutor Lesson Plan Series* book provides appropriate practice during tutoring sessions for learners for both face-to-face and online tutoring sessions focused on topics in Pre-Calculus.

The goal of the *Geometry: Math Tutor Lesson Plan Series* book is to support all types of tutors. Also, this book is to support teachers who want to provide in-class tutoring to their students in either an individualized or small group tutoring setting. Lastly, this book is also for teachers who are providing math intervention either individually or in small group tutoring sessions either face to face or online so that they can select the specific lesson plan to address the learner's math learning needs.

How to Use This Lesson Plan Book

iGlobal Educational Services, in collaboration with, Dr. Alicia Holland-Johnson, Tutor Expert and Consultant, created this tutoring resource to help with designing effective tutoring instruction for tutors and teachers who desire to provide in-class tutoring sessions.

These specific lessons were selected based upon field-tested experiences with learners who had learning needs over the years in these specific areas in mathematics. We have provided learning objectives and specific topics covered in each tutoring session so that you can align them with your state's specific standards or adapted standards. For overseas tutors, you can follow suite and align the lesson objectives to specific educational standards required in your country.

These lesson plans should be used to supplement a strong and viable curriculum that encourages differentiation for all diverse learners. They can be used in individual or small group tutoring sessions conducted face-to-face or online in any educational setting, including the classroom.

Organization of the Lesson Plan Book

Rather than provide a specific "curriculum" to follow, *Geometry: Math Tutor Lesson Plan Series* book provides a blueprint to design effective tutoring lessons that are aligned with the "*Dr. Holland-Johnson's Session Review Framework*". Tutor evaluators and coaches are able toanalyze tutoring sessions and coach tutors when utilizing the *"Dr. Holland-Johnson's Lesson Plan Blueprint for Tutors"*. In each lesson plan, learners have an opportunity to focus on real-world connections, vocabulary, and practice the math concepts learned in the tutoring sessions in the appropriate amounts to learn and retain the content knowledge. Tutors will have an opportunity to provide direct and guided instruction, while learners practice concepts on their own during independent instruction.

Each lesson plan comes with a mini-assessment pertaining to the math concepts learned in the specific tutoring session. Depending on the learner's academic needs, the tutor or teacher will deem when it is appropriate to administer the mini-assessment. For online tutoring sessions or as an online option to take the mini-assessment, tutors and teachers can upload these mini-assessments to be completed online in their choice of an online assessment tool.

Lesson 1
Triangles and Angle Relationships

Lesson Description

This lesson is designed to help students classify triangles based on their angles and sides. Additionally, students will learn how to describe angle relationships in triangles. Please be sure to utilize the questions to help spark student engagement and cover the vocabulary that is associated with this specific tutoring session. For your own knowledge, sample responses have been provided to guide you as well.

Learning Objectives

In today's lesson, the learners will classify triangles using their angles and sides in 3 out of 4 trials with at least 75% or higher accuracy.

Introduction

Triangles can be used in real word scenario. Suppose a ladder is leaning against a wall, the altitude of the ladder can be found by using the length of the ladder and the distance of the ladder from the wall by using Pythagorean Theorem because it makes a right-triangle. A triangular prism has an acute triangle at the front of the polyhedron shape because all the angles are less than 90 degrees.

Questions to Engage Students in Lesson

➤ What are different types of angles you know?

➤ Based on these angles, do you know how many types of triangles are there?

➤ What is the sum of angles of a triangle?

➤ Do you know the difference between interior and exterior angles of a triangle?

Connect Learning Objectives Student's Lives

Triangles and Angle relationships are widely used in:

A) Designing and Architecture.

B) Geometry and Trigonometry

C) Engineering and Other Sciences.

Specific Vocabulary Covered

Interior Angles of triangle

The inner angles of a triangle are interior angles.

Exterior Angles of triangle

The angles adjacent to the interior angles of a triangle are called exterior angles.

Acute Angled Triangle

A triangle having all angles less than 90° is an acute angled triangle.

Obtuse Angled Triangle

A triangle having one angle greater than 90° is an obtuse angled triangle.

Right Angled Triangle

A triangle having one angle cqual to 90° is a right angled triangle.

Equilateral Triangle

A triangle that has three congruent sides is an equilateral triangle.

Isosceles Triangle

A triangle that has two congruent sides is an isosceles triangle.

Scalene Triangle

A triangle that has all three sides of different length is a scalene triangle.

Direct & Guided Instruction: Modeling For You and Working With You

Classification of Triangles by Sides

1. **Equi Triangles**

   A triangle having three congruent sides is called an equilateral triangle.

2. **Isosceles Triangles**

   A triangle having two congruent sides is called an isosceles triangle.

3. **Scalene Triangles**

   A triangle having all three sides of different lengths is called a scalene triangle.

Classification of Triangles by Angles

1. **Acute Angled Triangle**

   A triangle that has all angles less than 90° is called acute angled triangle.

2. **Obtuse Angled Triangle**

   A triangle that has one angle greater than 90° is called obtuse angled triangle.

3. **Right Angled Triangle**

   A triangle that has one angle equal to 90° is called a right angled triangle.

4. **Equiangular Triangle**

   A triangle that has all angles equal to 60° is called an equiangular triangle. All three sides of an equiangular triangle are congruent.

Triangle Angles Relationship

1. **Triangle Angles Sum Theorem**

    The sum of all interior angles of a triangle is 180°.

2. **Exterior Angle Theorem**

    The measure of an exterior angle is equal to the sum of two non-adjacent interior angles of a triangle.

    In the figure, $m \angle A$ is an exterior angle and $m \angle B$ and $m \angle C$ are two non-adjacent angles,

    Therefore,

    $m \angle A = m \angle B + m \angle C$

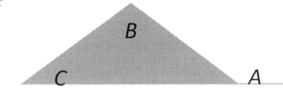

☞ <u>Problem 1:</u> **The measure of one interior angle of a right triangle is 37°. Find the measure of the unknown interior angle of the triangle?**

Teacher Questions

1. What is a right triangle?

2. How much is the sum of interior angles of a triangle?

3. How will you find the measure of unknown angle?

Solution

1. Let 'x' be the measure of unknown angle of the triangle.

    According to the triangle angle sum theorem,

    Sum of Interior angles of triangle = 180°

    $90 + 37 + x = 180°$

    $127 + x = 180°$

    $x = 180 - 127$

    $x = 53°$

☞ <u>**Problem 2:**</u> **If two adjacent interior angles are $(x + 1)°$ and $36°$ and their opposite exterior angle is $(3x + 5)°$. Find x and measure of exterior angle?**

Teacher Questions

1. Which theorem will be used to find the exterior angle of triangle?

2. What theorem of exterior angle states?

Solution

$x + 1 + 36 = 3x + 5$

$x + 37 = 3x + 5$

$37 - 5 = 3x - x$

$32 = 2x$

$x = 16$

Measure of Exterior Angle $= 3x + 5$

$$= 3(16) + 5$$

$$= 48 + 5 = 53°$$

☞ <u>**Problem 1:**</u> **Find the measures of angles of the given triangle?**

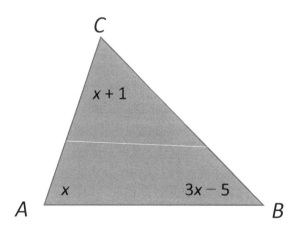

1. Are the angles shown in the figure interior or exterior?

2. What is the relationship between the interior angles of a triangle?

Solution

Using Triangle Angle Sum Theorem,

$$(x) + (3x - 5) + (x + 10) = 180°$$

$$x + 3x + x - 5 + 10 = 180°$$

$$5x + 5 = 180°$$

$$5x = 180 - 5$$

$$5x = 175$$

$$x = 175/5$$

$$x = m \angle A = 35°$$

$$m \angle B = 3x - 5 = 3(35) - 5 = 105 - 5 = 100°$$

$$m \angle C = x + 10 = 35 + 10 = 45°$$

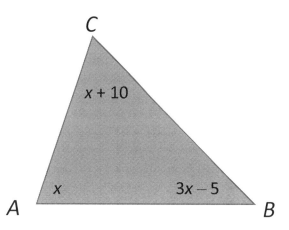

☞ **Problem 2:** Find x?

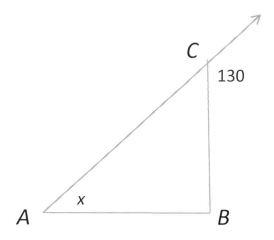

1. What is angle x is called?

2. What is angle labeled as 130° called?

3. Which angle relationship will you use to find x?

Solution

$m \angle$ B is 90°.

We know that measure of an exterior angle of a triangle is equal to the sum of two non adjacent interior angles. Therefore,

$130 = m \angle B + m \angle A$

$130 = x + 90$

$x = 130 - 90$

$x = 40°$

Video Suggestions

Please conduct a search on either YouTube or Teacher Tube to find appropriate videos for this lesson. Below are some suggested title searches:

➤ Triangle Angle Relationships

➤ Classification of Triangles

➤ Geometry and Trigonometry

➤ Interior and Exterior Angles of Triangle

Independent Instruction: Working On Your Own

Questions

☞ **Problem 1:** Find measures of the angles of the triangle given?

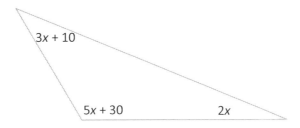

☞ **Problem 2:** Find the unknown interior angles of the triangle?

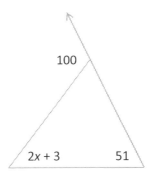

☞ **Problem 3:** Find $m \angle 1$, $m \angle 2$ and $m \angle 3$?

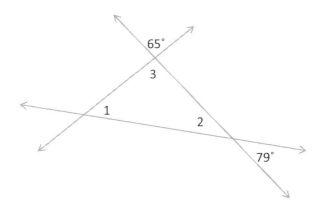

1. Using Triangle Sum Theorem,

    $3x + 10 + 5x + 30 + 2x = 180$

    $10x + 40 = 180$

    $10x = 180 - 40$

    $10x = 140$

    $x = 14$

    Hence the measures of angles of triangle are

    $2x = 2(14) = 28°$

    $(5x + 30) = 5(14) + 30 = 100°$

    $(3x + 10) = 3(14) + 10 = 52°$

2. Using Exterior angle theorem,

    $2x + 3 + 51 = 100$

    $2x + 54 = 100$

    $2x = 100 - 54$

    $2x = 46$

    $x = 23$

    Hence, the unknown interior angles are,

    Angle 1 = $(2x + 3) = 2(23) + 3 = 46 + 3 = 49°$

    Angle 2 = $180 - 51 - 49 = 80°$

3. As $m \angle 2$ and $79°$ are alternate angles, hence,

    $m \angle 2 = 79°$

    Also, $m \angle 3$ and $65°$ are alternate angles, hence,

    $m \angle 3 = 65°$

    Now,

    $m \angle 1 = 180 - m \angle 2 - m \angle 3$

    $m\angle 1 = 180 - 79 - 65$

    $m \angle 1 = 36°$

Mini-Assessment

☞ **Problem 1:** If two sides of a triangle are congruent
and one angle is obtuse the triangle is _____, _____.

   A. Obtuse, Scalene

   B. Obtuse, Equilateral

   C. Obtuse, Isosceles

   D. Obtuse, Equiangular

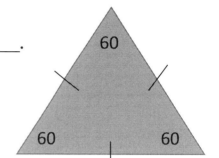

☞ **Problem 2:** Classify the triangle by its angles and sides.

   A. Acute, Scalene

   B. Acute, Isosceles

   C. Obtuse, equilateral

   D. Acute, Equilateral

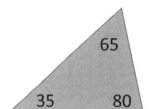

☞ **Problem 3:** Classify the triangle by its angles and sides.

   A. Acute, Equilateral

   B. Acute, Isosceles

   C. Acute, Scalene

   D. Acute, Equiangular

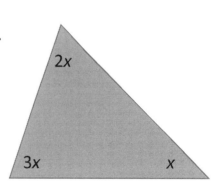

☞ **Problem 4:** : **Find *x*, if three angles of a triangle are given by,**

$$3x + 28, \ 5x + 52, \ 2x - 10$$

☞ **Problem 5:** **Find the measures of the angles of the triangle given and classify the triangle?**

☞ **Problem 6:** **Find measurment of the exterior angle of the triangle labeled as $(4x - 7)$?**

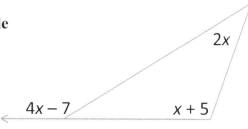

$2x$

$4x - 7$ $x + 5$

☞ **Problem 7: Find '*x*'?**

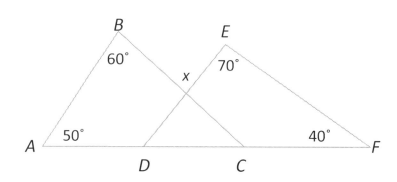

Mini-Assessment Answers and Explanations

1. Option C

2. Option D

3. Option C

4. $3x + 28 + 5x + 52 + 2x - 10 = 180$

$10x + 70 = 180$

$10x = 180 - 70$

$10x = 110$

$x = 11$

5. $x + 2x + 3x = 180$

$6x = 180$

$x = 180/6 = 30$

Therefore, Angles of triangle are

$x = 30$

$2x = 2(30) = 60$

$3x = 3(30) = 90$

Triangle is a right angled triangle.

6. $4x - 7 = 2x + x + 5$

$4x - 7 = 3x + 5$

$4x - 3x = 5 + 7$

$x = 12$

Exterior Angle $= 4x - 7 = 4(12) - 7 = 48 - 7 = 41°$

7. In Triangle *ABC*

$\angle C = 180 - 60 - 50 = 70$

In Triangle *DEF*

$\angle D = 180 - 70 - 40 = 70$

In Triangle *DCG*

$\angle G = 180 - \angle D - \angle C = 180 - 70 - 70 = 40$

We can see that the Angle *DGC* and Angle *BGE* are alternate angles, so they must be congruent,

$\angle BGE = \angle DGC$

$x = 40°$

Lesson Reflection

Classification of Triangles by Sides

1. **Equilateral Triangles**

   A triangle having three congruent sides is called an equilateral triangle.

2. **Isosceles Triangles**

   A triangle having two congruent sides is called an isosceles triangle.

3. **Scalene Triangles**

   A triangle having all three sides of different lengths is called a scalene triangle.

Classification of Triangles by Angles

1. **Acute Angled Triangle**

   A triangle that has all angles less than 90° is called acute angled triangle.

2. **Obtuse Angled Triangle**

   A triangle that has one angle greater than 90° is called obtuse angled triangle.

3. **Right Angled Triangle**

   A triangle that has one angle equal to 90° is called a right angled triangle.

4. **Equiangular Triangle**

   A triangle that has all angles equal to 60° is called an equiangular triangle. All three sides of an equiangular triangle are congruent.

Triangle Angles Relationship

1. **Triangle Sum Theorem**

   The sum of all interior angles of a triangle is 180°.

2. **Exterior Angle Theorem**

   The measure of an exterior angle is equal to the sum of two non adjacent interior angles of a triangle.

Lesson 2
Triangle Congruence

Lesson Description:

This lesson is designed to help students describe triangle congruence by using a variety of Theorems. Please be sure to utilize the questions to help spark student engagement and cover the vocabulary that is associated with this specific tutoring session. For your own knowledge, sample responses have been provided to guide you as well.

Learning Objective(s):

In today's lesson, the learner will describe triangle congruence by using a variety of Theorems in 3 out of 4 trials with at least 75% accuracy or above.

Introduction

Triangle congruency can be used in real word problems. A civil engineer can use the congruency of the triangles to find the dimensions of the triangular roof of a building using the fact that the triangles are congruent if three sides and angles are exactly the same. If the sides of two triangles are exactly the same then the triangles must be congruent because the angles must also be the same.

Questions to Engage Students in Lesson

1. What is meant by congruence?

2. How many parts a triangle has?

3. In your own words how would you describe congruence of triangles?

4. If a transversal intersects two parallel lines what will be the relation between alternate interior angles formed?

5. What are the opposite angles made by two intersecting lines and how they are related?

Connect Learning Objectives Student's Lives

Triangles congruence are used,

A. In designing and constructing Bridges, buildings, etc.

B. In architectural designs and drawings.

C. Used in Science for example, mineral design, rock formation, crystal formation etc.

Specific Vocabulary Covered

Triangles Congruence

Two triangles are congruent if their corresponding sides are equal in length and their corresponding angles are equal in size.

Postulate

A truth, a reality or an axiom that is used as a basis of reasoning.

Corresponding Parts of Congruent Triangles

A pair of sides or angles of two triangles that have the same relative position in the triangles.

Hypotenuse

The side of a right triangle that is opposite to the right angle is called hypotenuse.

Leg of Right Triangle

Two sides that make the right angle of a right triangle are called legs of the right triangle.

Direct & Guided Instruction: Modeling For You and Working With You

Triangle Congruence SSS and SAS

SSS Postulate

If all three sides of a triangle are congruent to the corresponding sides of the other triangle, then triangles are congruent by SSS Postulate.

SAS Postulate

If any two sides and their included angle of a triangle are congruent to the corresponding sides and their included angle, then triangles are congruent by SAS Postulate.

Triangle Congruence ASA, AAS and HL

ASA Postulate

➤ ASA Stands for 'Angle-Side-Angle'.

➤ If any two angles and their included side of a triangle are congruent to the corresponding two angles and their included side of another triangle, then the triangles are congruent by ASA postulate.

AAS Postulate

➤ AAS Stands for 'Angle-Angle-Side'.

➤ If any two angles and an opposite side of a triangle are congruent to the corresponding two angles and opposite side of another triangle, then triangles are congruent by AAS postulate.

HL Postulate

➤ HL Stands for 'Hypotenuse-Leg'.

➤ If in a right triangle a hypotenuse and a leg are congruent to the hypotenuse and a leg of another right triangle, then both the right triangles are congruent by HL Postulate.

Triangle Congruence CPCTC

➤ CPCTC Stands for 'Corresponding Parts of Congruent Triangles are Congruent'.

➤ If there are two triangles and they are proved congruent then by CPCTC Postulate all other corresponding parts of the triangles are congruent.

☞ **Problem 1:** Write congruence statement between the triangles and state the postulate applied?

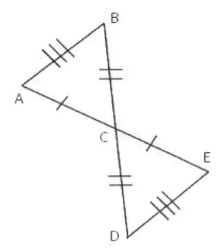

1. Write the statement for first pair of corresponding congruent sides?

2. Write the congruence statement for second pair of corresponding congruent sides?

3. Write the congruence statement for third pair of corresponding congruent sides?

4. Which postulate will be used to prove the triangles congruent?

Solution

$AC \cong CE$

$CB \cong CD$

$BA \cong DE$

Using SSS Postulate Congruence statement for triangles can be written as,

$\triangle ACB \cong \triangle ECD$

☞ **Problem 2:** **Is it possible to prove the triangles congruent, If so state the postulate and write the congruence statement?**

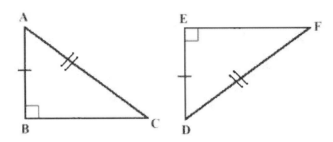

Teacher Questions

1. Write the congruence statements forthe pairs of corresponding sides of the triangles?

2. What type of both the triangles are?

3. Can you guess the postulate that can be used to prove the triangles congruence?

Solution

$\angle B \cong \angle E = 90°$

$AB \cong DE$ (Hypotenuse)

$AC \cong DF$ (Leg)

By Hypotenuse-Leg Postulate, triangles are congruent. The congruency statement can be written as,

$\triangle ABC \cong \triangle DEF$

☞ **Problem 1:** Given that $AC \cong BC$ and $\angle ADC \cong \angle BDC \cong 90°$. Prove that $\angle A \cong \angle B$.

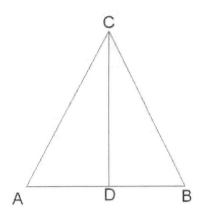

1. How can we prove two angles from two different triangles are congruent?

2. When is CPCTC is used?

3. Is there any way to prove the triangles congruent?

Solution

Statements	Reasons
$\angle ADC \cong \angle BDC \cong 90°$	Both are right triangles.
$AC \cong BC$	Given (Hypotenuse)
$CD \cong CD$	Common Side (Leg)
$\triangle ADC \cong \triangle BDC$	HL Postulate
$\angle A \cong \angle B$	CPCTC Postulate

☞ <u>**Problem 2:**</u> **Given that** $AR \cong BR$ **and** $PR \cong QR$ **Prove that** $AP \cong BQ$?

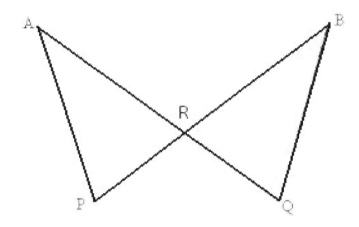

Teacher Questions

1. How can we prove two line segments from two different triangles are congruent?

2. When is CPCTC is used?

3. What are alternate angles and how are they related?

4. Is there any way to prove the triangles congruent?

Solution

Statements	Reasons
$AR \cong BR$	Given
$\angle ARP \cong \angle BRQ$	Vertical Angles
$PR \cong QR$	Given
$\triangle ARP \cong \triangle BRQ$	SAS Postulate
$AP \cong BQ$	CPCTC Postulate

Video Suggestions

Please conduct a search on either YouTube or Teacher Tube to find appropriate videos for this lesson. Below are some suggested title searches:

➤ Triangle Congruence

➤ Congruent Triangles by SSS and SAS

➤ CPCTC

Independent Instruction: Working on Your Own

Questions

☞ <u>**Problem 1:**</u> Given two triangles $\triangle ABC$ and $\triangle XYZ$. Find out the triangles are congruent or not? State the postulate if congruent?

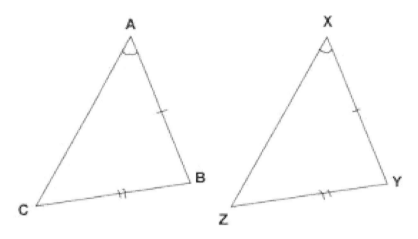

☞ <u>**Problem 2:**</u> Given that $AC \cong BC$ and $CE \cong CD$, then prove that $AD \cong BE$?

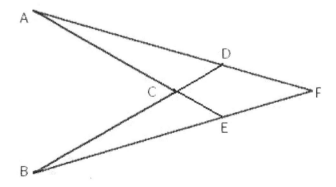

☞ **Problem 3:** Given that $OS \cong OP$, then prove that $OR \cong OQ$?

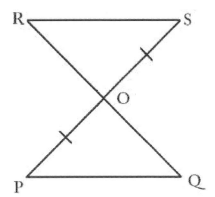

Solution

1.

Statements	Reasons
$BC \cong XZ$	Given
$AB \cong XY$	Given
$\angle A \cong \angle X$	Given

There is no such postulate like SSA for triangles congruence. Hence given triangles are not congruent.

2.

Statements	Reasons
$AC \cong BC$	Given
$\angle ACD \cong \angle BCE$	Vertical Angles
$CE \cong CD$	Given
$\triangle ACD \cong \triangle BCE$	SAS Postulate
$AD \cong BE$	CPCTC Postulate

3.

Statements	Reasons
$\angle S \cong \angle P$	Alternate Interior Angles
$OS \cong OP$	Given
$\angle SOR \cong \angle POQ$	Vertical Angles
$\triangle SOR \cong \triangle POQ$	ASA Postulate
$OR \cong OQ$	CPCTC Postulate

Mini-Assessment

☞ **Problem 1:** The postulate that cannot be used to prove the triangles congruent is,

A. HL Postulate   **B.** SAS Postulate   **C.** AAS Postulate

D. SSA Postulate   **E.** SSS Postulate

☞ **Problem 2:** The triangles shown in the figure are congruent. The postulate used to prove the triangle congruent is,

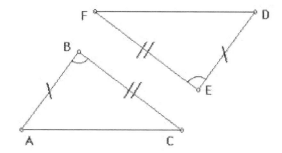

A. SSS Postulate   **B.** ASA Postulate   **C.** AAS Postulate

D. SSA Postulate   **E.** SAS Postulate

☞ **Problem 3:** If $\triangle ABC \cong \triangle XYZ$, which one of the following statements is not true?

A. $\angle A \cong \angle X$ **B.** $\angle B \cong \angle Y$ **C.** $\angle A \cong \angle Y$

D. $\angle Z \cong \angle C$ **E.** $AB \cong XY$

☞ **Problem 4:** Given that $\angle C \cong \angle B$ and $AB \parallel CD$. Prove that, $AB \cong CD$?

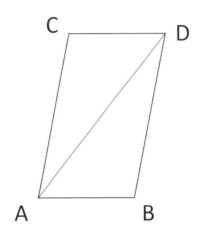

☞ **Problem 5:** Given that $BC \cong CE$ and $AB \parallel ED$, Prove that, $AC \cong CD$?

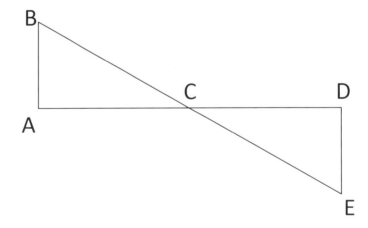

☞ **Problem 6:** Given that *BC* ≅ *CE* and *AC* ≅ *DC*, Prove that *AB* ≅ *DE*?

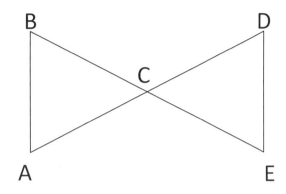

☞ **Problem 7:** Given that *PR* ≅ *QS*, Prove that, ∠*P* ≅ ∠*S*?

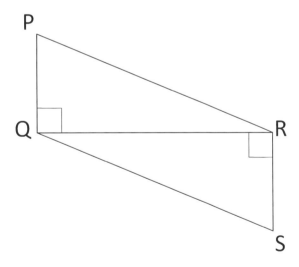

Mini-Assessment Answers and Explanations

1. Option D

2. Option E

3. Option C

4.

Statements	Reasons
$\angle C \cong \angle B$	Given
$\angle CDA \cong \angle DAB$	Alternate interior Angles, as $AB \parallel CD$ (given)
$AD \cong AD$	Common Side
$\triangle ABD \cong \triangle DCA$	AAS Postulate
$AB \cong CD$	CPCTC Postulate

5.

Statements	Reasons
$BC \cong CE$	Given
$\angle B \cong \angle E$	Alternate interior Angles, as $AB \parallel ED$ (given)
$\angle BCA \cong \angle DCE$	Vertical angles
$\triangle ABC \cong \triangle DEC$	ASA Postulate
$AC \cong CD$	CPCTC Postulate

6.

Statements	Reasons
$BC \cong CE$	Given
$\angle BCA \cong \angle DCE$	Vertical Angles
$AC \cong DC$	Given
$\triangle ABC \cong \triangle DEC$	SAS Postulate
$AB \cong DE$	CPCTC Postulate

7. **Statements**   **Reasons**

$PR \cong QS$ Given

$\angle PQR \cong \angle SRQ = 90°$ Given

$QR \cong QR$ Common Side

$\triangle PQR \cong \triangle SRQ$ HL Postulate

$\angle P \cong \angle S$ CPCTC Postulate

Lesson Reflection

Triangle Congruence Postulates

SSS Postulate

If all three sides of a triangle are congruent to the corresponding sides of the other triangle, then triangles are congruent by SSS Postulate.

SAS Postulate

If any two sides and their included angle of a triangle are congruent to the corresponding sides and their included angle, then triangles are congruent by SAS Postulate.

ASA Postulate

➤ ASA Stands for 'Angle-Side-Angle'.

➤ If any two angles and their included side of a triangle are congruent to the corresponding two angles and their included side of another triangle, then the triangles are congruent by ASA postulate.

AAS Postulate

➤ AAS Stands for 'Angle-Angle-Side'.

➤ If any two angles and an opposite side of a triangle are congruent to the corresponding two angles and opposite side of another triangle, then triangles are congruent by AAS postulate.

HL Postulate

➤ HL Stands for 'Hypotenuse-Leg'.

➤ If in a right triangle a hypotenuse and a leg are congruent to the hypotenuse and a leg of another right triangle, then both the right triangles are congruent by HL Postulate.

CPCTC

➤ CPCTC Stands for 'Corresponding Parts of Congruent Triangles are Congruent'.

➤ If there are two triangles and they are proved congruent then by CPCTC Postulate all other corresponding parts of the triangles are congruent.

Lesson 3
Trigonometric Ratios

Lesson Description

This lesson is designed to help students solve right triangles using trigonometric ratios. Please be sure to utilize the questions to help spark student engagement and cover the vocabulary that is associated with this specific tutoring session. For your own knowledge, sample responses have been provided to guide you as well.

Learning Objectives

In today's lesson, the learner will solve right triangles using trigonometric ratios with 3 out of 4 trials with 75% or above accuracy.

Introduction

Trigonometric ratios are: $\sin \theta = \frac{Opposite}{Hypotenuse}$, $\cos \theta = \frac{Adjacent}{Hypotenuse}$, and $\tan \theta = \frac{Opposite}{Adjacent}$.

Trigonometric ratios have wide real world applications. Suppose a person is looking at the top of the building standing at a distance from the building, we can use trigonometric ratios to find the height of the building if we know the distance of the building from the person and the angle of elevation between the line of sight and the top of the building.

Questions to Engage Students in Lesson

➤ What is a right triangle?

➤ If any two angles of a triangle are known, is there any way to find the third angle?

➤ If you know any one angle of a right triangle other than the right angle, can you find the other angle?

➤ If you know length of two sides of a right triangle, can you calculate the length of the third side?

Connect Learning Objectives Student's Lives

Trigonometric ratios are used

A) In forestry to determine the heights of the trees.

B) In real life to determine the distance an airplane travels as it is taking off, or the distance a skier travels as they ski down a mountain.

C) In Physics for example, Vectors applications.

D) In Astronomy to find the distance between the stars.

E) In Engineering to develop some object according to the specific measurements.

Specific Vocabulary Covered

Similar triangles

Two triangles are similar if their corresponding angles are congruent and their corresponding sides are proportional.

Right Triangle

A triangle is a right triangle if one of its angles measures 90°.

Pythagorean Theorem

Pythagorean theorem states that in a right triangle the square of hypotenuse is equal to the sum of the square of the other two sides.

Triangle Sum Theorem

Triangle sum theorem states that sum of all three angles of a triangle is 180°.

Trigonometric Ratios

Trigonometric ratios are the ratios that describe the relationship between an angle and two sides of the right triangle.

Direct & Guided Instruction: Modeling For You and Working With You

Similarity in Right Triangles

Similar Triangles

Two triangles are similar if their corresponding side are proportional and their corresponding angles are congruent.

If a, b and c are lengths of one triangle and x, y and z are corresponding lengths of other triangle, assuming that both the triangles have congruent corresponding angles, then for similar triangles,

$$\frac{a}{x} = \frac{b}{y} = \frac{c}{z} = constant$$

Theorem

The altitude to the hypotenuse divides the right triangle in to two right triangles that are similar to the original triangle and to each other as well.

Explanation:

In the figure the altitude BD divides the triangles into two triangles making all three triangles similar to each other.

Similarity of $\triangle ADB$ and $\triangle CDB$ can be shown as,

$$\frac{AD}{CD} = \frac{AB}{CB} = \frac{BD}{BD}$$

Similarity of $\triangle ADB$ and $\triangle ABC$ can be shown as,

$$\frac{AB}{BD} = \frac{BC}{AD} = \frac{AC}{AB}$$

Similarity of $\triangle BDC$ and $\triangle ABC$ can be shown as,

$$\frac{AB}{BD} = \frac{BC}{DC} = \frac{AC}{BC}$$

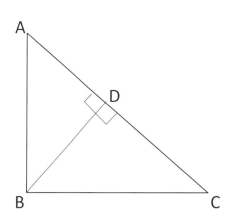

39

Geometric Mean Theorems for Similar Triangles

Theorem 1:

The length of altitude is the geometric mean of the lengths of the two segments of the hypotenuse.

$(AD)(CD) = (BD)^2$

$$\frac{AD}{BD} = \frac{BD}{CD}$$

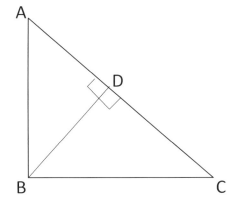

Theorem 2:

The length of each leg of the right triangle is the geometric mean of the lengths of hypotenuse and the segment of the hypotenuse that is adjacent to that leg.

$(AC)(DC) = (BC)^2$

$$\frac{AC}{BC} = \frac{BC}{DC}$$

Trigonometric Ratios

$$Sin\,\theta = \frac{Opposite}{Hypotenuse}$$

$$Cos\,\theta = \frac{Adjacent}{Hypotenuse}$$

$$Tan\,\theta = \frac{Opposite}{Adjacent}$$

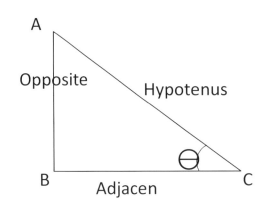

Trigonometric ratios can be remembered as *SOH, CAH, TOA*.

Solving Right Triangles

Finding the unknown parts of a right triangle is called solving a right triangle.

How to Solve a Right Triangle

To solve a right triangle, three rules are used,

1. The trigonometric Ratios

2. Pythagorean Theorem

3. Triangle angle Sum Theorem

☞ **Problem 1:** Find the value of x?

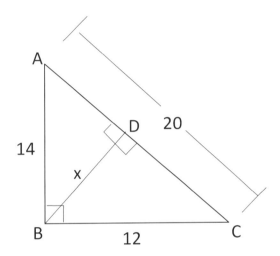

1. What type of triangle ABC is?

2. BD is an altitude to the hypotenuse AC, dividing the triangle into two triangles.

Can you relate new triangles to the original triangle?

3. Can you identify any other pair of similar triangles?

Solution

To find 'x', we will write a similarity statement between $\triangle ABC$ and $\triangle ADB$,

$$\frac{x}{12} = \frac{12}{20}$$

$$x = \frac{12 \times 12}{20}$$

$$x = \frac{36}{5}$$

☞ **Problem 2: Solve the right triangle *XYZ*?**

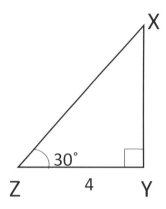

Teacher Questions:

1. What is meant by solving a triangle?

2. Which trigonometric function will be used to calculate the value of *XY*?

3. Which trigonometric ratio will be used to find *XZ*?

4. Is there any other way to find value of *XZ* when *XY* and *YZ* is known?

5. Which theorem will be used to calculate the value of ∠*X*?

Solution

$$Tan\,\theta = \frac{Opposite}{Adjacent}$$

$$Tan\,30 = \frac{XY}{4}$$

$$XY = (Tan\,30)(4) = (0.577)(4) = 2.309$$

$$Sin\,\theta = \frac{XY}{XZ}$$

$$Sin\,30 = \frac{2.309}{XZ}$$

$$XZ = \frac{2.309}{Sin\,30} = \frac{2.309}{0.5} = 4.618$$

Using triangle sum theorem,

$$\angle X + \angle Y + \angle Z = 180$$

$$\angle X = 180 - \angle Y - \angle Z = 180 - 90 - 30 - 60°$$

👉 **Problem 1:** Find x?

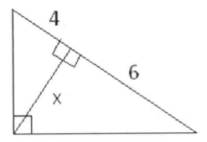

Teacher Questions

1. What is 'x' in the given figure?

2. What strategy will you use to find 'x'?

3. State the theorem that will be used to find 'x'?

Solution

$$\frac{4}{x} = \frac{x}{6}$$

$$(4)(6) = x^2$$

$$24 = x^2$$

$$x = \sqrt{24} = 2\sqrt{6}$$

☞ **Problem 2: Solve the triangle.**

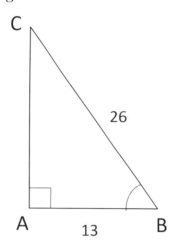

Teacher Questions:

1. Length of two sides are given, how will you find the length of third side?

2. Which trigonometric ratio will be used to find the base angle?

3. Which theorem will you use to find the measure of third angle?

Solution

Using Pythagorean theorem to find AC,

$(BC)^2 = (AC)^2 + (AB)^2$

$(26)^2 = (AC)^2 + (13)^2$

$676 = (AC)^2 + 169$

$(AC)^2 = 676 - 169 = 507$

$AC = 22.52$

Using Cosine ratio to find $\angle B$,

Cos B = Adjacent / Hypotenuse

Cos B = 13/ 26 = 0.5

$\angle B = 60°$

Using Triangle angle sum theorem to find $\angle C$

$\angle C = 180 - \angle A - \angle B$

$\angle C = 180 - 90 - 60$

$\angle C = 30°$

Video Suggestions

Please conduct a search on either YouTube or Teacher Tube to find appropriate videos for this lesson. Below are some suggested title searches:

➤ Similar Triangles

➤ Geometry – Sine Cosine and Tangent Ratios

➤ Trigonometric Ratios in Right Triangle

➤ Solve right Triangles Part 1 Basics

Independent Instruction: Working On Your Own

Questions

☞ **Problem 1:** Find '*x*'?

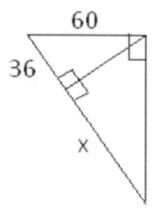

☞ **Problem 2:** Solve the triangle?

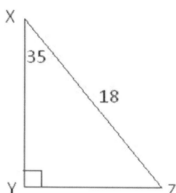

☞ **Problem 3:** Solve the triangle.

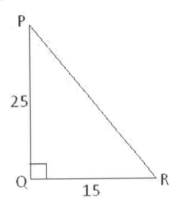

Solution

1. $$\frac{x+36}{60} = \frac{60}{36}$$

$$x+36 = \frac{60 \times 60}{36}$$

$$x+36 = \frac{3600}{36}$$

$$x+36 = 100$$

$$x = 100 - 36$$

$$x = 64$$

2. Using Triangle Sum theorem,

$\angle Z = 180 - 90 - 35$

$\angle Z = 55$

Using Cosine ratio to find YZ,

Cos Z = Adjacent/Hypotenuse

Cos 55 = YZ / 18

$YZ = 18 * $ Cos 55

$YZ = 18 * (0.5736) = 10.32$

Using Sine Ratio to find XY,

Sin Z = Opposite/Hypotenuse

Sin 55 = XY / 18

$XY = 18 * $ Sin 55

$XY = 18 * (0.8191) = 14.74$

3. Using Pythagorean theorem to find PR,

$(PR)^2 = (PQ)^2 + (QR)^2$

$(PR)^2 = (25)^2 + (15)^2$

$(PR)^2 = 625 + 225$

$(PR)2 = 850$

$PR = 29.15$

Using Tangent ratio to find $\angle R$,

Tan R = Opposite/Adjacent

Tan R = 25/15 = 1.67

$R = 59.03°$

Using triangle angle sum theorem to find $\angle P$,

$\angle P = 180 - \angle Q - \angle R$

$\angle P = 180 - 90 - 59.03$

$\angle P = 30.97°$

Mini-Assessment

☞ <u>**Problem 1:**</u> In $\triangle LMN$, $LN = 16$ and $MN = 8$, What will be the measure of $\angle LNM$?

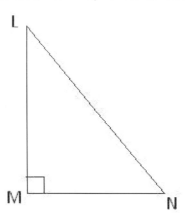

A. 30 **B.** 45 **C.** 55

D. 60 **E.** Cannot be determined

☞ <u>**Problem 2:**</u> Find the length of the side AB?

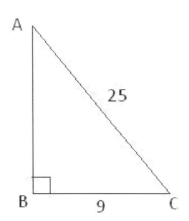

A. 16 **B.** 5.83 **C.** 4

D. 2.78 **E.** Cannot be determined

☞ **Problem 3:** : Find *x*, if ∆*ABC* and ∆*AED* are similar triangles?

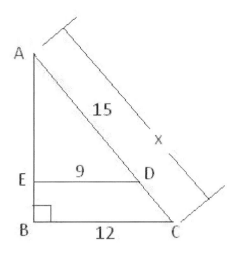

A. 5   **B.** 7.2   **C.** 11.2   **D.** 12   **E.** 20

☞ **Problem 4:** Find the value of *x* and *y*?

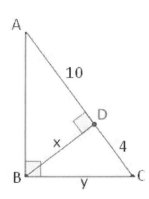

☞ **Problem 5:** Solve the triangle?

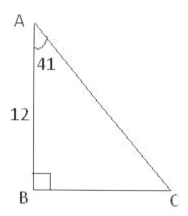

☞ **Problem 6:** Solve the triangle?

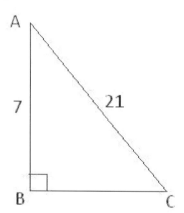

☞ **Problem 7:** A 15 ft long ladder is leaning against the wall. If the foot of the ladder is 8 ft away from the wall, find the measure of angle the ladder is making with the ground. Also find the distance, the ladder reaches on the wall?

Mini-Assessment Answers and Explanations

1. Option D

2. Option E

3. Option E

4. $10/x = x/4$

   $X^2 = 40$

   $X = 6.32$

   To find 'y'
   $4/y = y/(10+4)$
   $4/y = y/14$
   $y2 = 56$
   $y = 7.48$

5. We will find third angle of the triangle first using triangle sum theorem,

   $\angle C = 180 - 90 - 41$
   $\angle C = 49°$

   Now, Tan C = Opposite / Adjacent
   Tan 49 = $12 / BC$
   $BC = 12/$ Tan 49
   $BC = 12/ 1.15$
   $BC = 10.43$

   To find AC lets use the sine ratio,
   Sin C = Opposite/Hypotenuse
   Sin 49 = $12 / AC$
   $AC = 12 / $ Sin 49
   $AC = 12 / 0.75$
   $AC = 15.9$

6. Use Pythagorean theorem to find third side of the right angle,

$$(AC)^2 = (AB)^2 + (BC)^2$$

$$(21)^2 = (7)^2 + (BC)^2$$

$$441 = 49 + (BC)^2$$

$$(BC)^2 = 441 - 49 = 392$$

$$BC = 19.8$$

Using Sine Ratio to find $\angle C$,

Sin C = Opposite / Hypotenuse

Sin C = 7/21

Sin C = 0.33

C = 19.47°

Using Triangle sum theorem to find $\angle A$,

$$\angle A = 180 - \angle B - \angle C$$

$$\angle A = 180 - 90 - 19.47$$

$$\angle A = 70.53°$$

7. Draw a diagram for the situation given.

Hypotenuse = 15 ft

Adjacent = 8 ft

Angle with the ground = θ = ?

Cos θ = Adjacent / Hypotenuse

Cos θ = 8 / 15

Cos θ = 0.53

θ = 57.77°

Lesson Reflection

Theorems for Similar Triangles

Theorem

➤ The altitude to the hypotenuse divides the right triangle in to two right triangles that are similar to the original triangle and to each other as well.

➤ The length of altitude is the geometric mean of the lengths of the two segments of the hypotenuse.

➤ The length of each leg of the right triangle is the geometric mean of the lengths of hypotenuse and the segment of the hypotenuse that is adjacent to that leg.

Direct Instruction

Solving Right Triangles

To solve a right triangle, three rules are used,

1. The trigonometric Ratios
2. Pythagorean Theorem
3. Triangle angle Sum Theorem

Trigonometric Ratios

$$Sin\,\theta = \frac{Opposite}{Hypotenuse}$$

$$Cos\,\theta = \frac{Adjacent}{Hypotenuse}$$

$$Tan\,\theta = \frac{Opposite}{Adjacent}$$

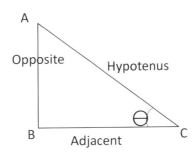

Lesson 4
Applying Trigonometric Ratios

Lesson Description:

This lesson is designed for learners to apply trigonometric ratios. Additionally, learners will have an opportunity to explore Angles of Elevation and Depression, Laws of Sines and Cosines, and Vectors. Please be sure to utilize the questions to help spark student engagement and cover the vocabulary that is associated with this specific tutoring session. For your own knowledge, sample responses have been provided to guide you as well.

Learning Objective(s):

In today's lesson, the learner will apply trigonometric ratios in 3 out of 4 trials with at least 75% or above accuracy.

Introduction

The concept of trigonometric ratios can be applied to real world problems. Trigonometric ratios are used to build a ramp to load cards from the back of the truck. We can find the length of the ramp if we can find the height of bed of the truck and the angle of elevation between the ground and the bed of the truck. It will become easier to load the cars in the truck in that way if we can find all the required measurements using trigonometric ratios.

Questions to Engage Students in Lesson

1. You know the opposite and the adjacent of a right triangle. Which one of the trigonometric ratio will be effective to find the base angle?

2. If you know the Hypotenuse and Opposite of a right triangle, which procedure will you follow to find Adjacent?

3. In your own words how will you describe an oblique triangle?

Insert Question to Engage Students in Lesson

1. You know the opposite and the adjacent of a right triangle. Which one of the trigonometric ratio will be effective to find the base angle?

2. If you know the Hypotenuse and Opposite of a right triangle, which procedure will you follow to find Adjacent?

3. In your own words how will you describe an oblique triangle?

Connect Learning Objectives Student's Lives

Trigonometric Ratios and Sine and Cosine Laws are used,

A) To use in land surveying by Surveyors.

B) To complete their missions in space as well as by pilots while landing, taking off and navigation etc by Astronauts.

C) To calculate the elevations of the mountains for hiking.

Specific Vocabulary Covered

Line of Sight

Line of sight is a straight line made by the eye of the observer and the object.

Angle of Elevation

When an observer looks up, the angle between the line of sight and the horizontal line is called angle of elevation.

Angle of Depression

When an observer looks down, the angle between the line of sight and the horizontal line is called angle of depression.

Oblique Triangle

A triangle having no right angle is called an oblique triangle. Acute and obtuse angled triangles are oblique triangles.

Vector

A vector is a quantity that has magnitude and direction.

Magnitude of Vector

Magnitude of a vector is the distance between the initial point to the terminal point of the vector.

Equal Vectors

Two vectors are said to be equal if they have same magnitude and direction. For two vectors to be equal it is not necessary that they have same initial and terminal points.

Parallel Vectors

If two vectors have same or opposite directions, they are parallel vectors. The magnitudes of parallel vectors may differ.

Direct & Guided Instruction: Modeling For You and Working With You

Angles of Elevation and Depression

Angle of Elevation

If an object is above the observer, the angle made by the eye of the observer to the horizontal line in order to look up at the object is called the angle of elevation.

Angle of Depression

If an object is below the observer, the angle made by the eye of the observer to the horizontal line in order to look down at the object is called the angle of depression.

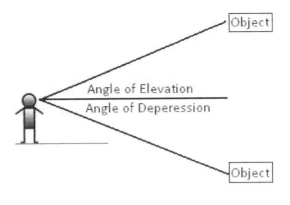

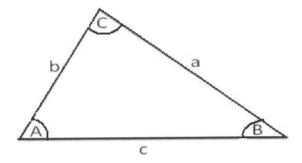

Law of Sines and Cosines

Laws of Sines and Cosines are used to solve the oblique triangles.

Laws of Sines

Law of Sines is best to use when,

(i). Two angles and a side opposite to one of the angles are known (SAA).

(ii). Two angles and their included side are given (ASA).

(iii). Two sides and an angle opposite to the given sides are known (SSA).

Laws of Sines are stated as:

$$\frac{a}{Sin\,A} = \frac{b}{Sin\,B} = \frac{c}{Sin\,C}$$

Laws of Cosines

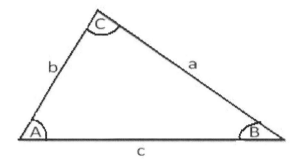

Laws of Cosines are best to use when,

(i). Two sides and the angle between them are given (SAS).

(ii). All three sides are known (SSS).

Laws of Cosines are stated as:

$$a^2 = b^2 + c^2 - 2bc.Cos(A)$$
$$b^2 = a^2 + c^2 - 2ac.Cos(B)$$
$$c^2 = a^2 + b^2 - 2ab.Cos(C)$$

The Ambiguous Case (SSA)

When two sides and an angle opposite to one of them is given, there arises three cases.

(i). No such triangle exist.

(ii). The triangle is a right triangle.

(iii). There could be one or two possible right triangles.

Value of Sin A	Solution Triangle
Sin $A > 1$	No triangle Exist.
Sin $A = 1$	Right Triangle
Sin $A < 1$	One or two possible triangles

Vectors

A vector is a quantity that has a magnitude and direction. A vector 'u' can be written as

Magnitude of Vector

The magnitude of a vector shown in a coordinate plane can be calculated using distance formula. The magnitude of a vector u can be denoted as

Direction of Vector

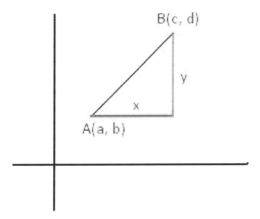

The direction of a vector can be found by calculating the angle of the vector to the horizontal line. A vector with an initial point A and terminal B is shown in the figure. Its direction can be calculated

as, $Tan^{-1}\left(\dfrac{y}{x}\right)$

A vector is written in a component form using initial and terminal point as, $(a-c, b-d)$.

Adding Vectors

Two vectors $\vec{u}_1 = (x_1, y_1)$ and $\vec{u}_2 = (x_2, y_2)$ can be added as,

$$\vec{u}_1 + \vec{u}_2 = (x_1, y_1) + (x_2, y_2)$$
$$\vec{u}_1 + \vec{u}_2 = (x_1 + x_2, y_1 + y_2)$$

☞ **Problem 1:** A man is standing 12 meters away from a tree. The angle of elevation from the man's feet to the top of the tree is 33°. What will be the height of the tree?

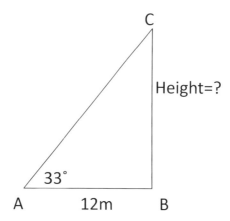

Teacher Questions

1. What should be the first step that will help us visualize the situation?

2. Where will be the angle of elevation, on the base or on the top of the tree?

3. Which trigonometric ratio will you use to find the height of the tree?

Solution

$$Tan\ A = \frac{BC}{AB}$$

$$Tan\ 33 = \frac{BC}{12}$$

$$BC = 12 * (Tan\ 33)$$

$$BC = 12 * (0.6494) = 7.7929$$

Therefore,

Height of Tree = 7.7929 m

☞ **Problem 2:** If initial point of a vector is (3, 5) and terminal point is (–5, –1). Find the vector in the terminal form, its magnitude and direction?

1. What is a vector?

2. How to find a vector when its initial and terminal points are known?

3. Which formula is used to find the magnitude of the vector when its initial and terminal points are given on a coordinate plane?

4. Which trigonometric ratio is used to find the direction of the vector?

Solution

Initial point = (3, 5)

Terminal point = (–5, –1)

Vector = (3 + 5, 5 +1) = (8, 6)

Magnitude of Vector = $\sqrt{(3+5)^2+(5+1)^2} = \sqrt{8^2+6^2} = \sqrt{64+36} = \sqrt{100} = 10$

$$Tan^{-1}\left(\frac{y}{x}\right)$$

Direction of Vector = $Tan^{-1}\left(\frac{6}{8}\right) = 36.87°$

☞ **Problem 1: Solve the triangle.**

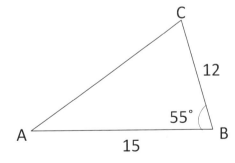

Teacher Questions

1. What type of triangle the given triangle is?

2. How we solve oblique triangles?

3. When two sides and their included angle is given, which law is suitable to use?

4. How to find Angle *A* and Angle *C*?

Solution

Using Cosine Law,

$$b^2 = a^2 + c^2 - 2acCosB$$

$$b^2 = (12)^2 + (15)^2 - 2(12)(15)Cos55°$$

$$b^2 = 144 + 225 - 206.49$$

$$b^2 = 162.51 \Rightarrow b = 12.75$$

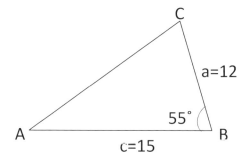

Using Sine Law to find Angle *A*,

$$\frac{a}{Sin\,A} = \frac{b}{Sin\,B}$$

$$\frac{12}{Sin\,A} = \frac{12.75}{Sin\,55°}$$

$$Sin\,A = \frac{12 \times Sin\,55°}{12.75} = 0.77$$

$$A = 50.44°$$

Now, $\angle C = 180 - \angle A - \angle B = 180 - 50.44 - 55 = 74.56°$

☞ **Problem 2:** Angles of depression of two ships from the top of a light pole are 15° and 35°. The light pole is 25m high. Find the Distance between the ships if they are at the same side of the light pole?

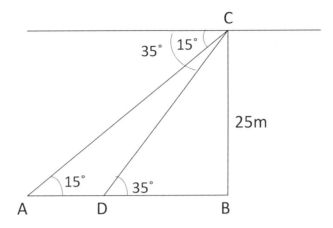

Teacher Questions

1. Name the two lines that make the angle of depression?

2. For angle of depression, will the horizontal line be at the top of the pole or at the base of the pole?

3. Name the pair of angles of parallel lines, that are used to find the angle of the triangle using angle of depression?

Solution

Let one ship is at point A and other ship is at Point D. The distance between the ships is AD.

In $\triangle ABC$, $Tan\ A = \dfrac{BC}{AB}$

$Tan\ 15° = \dfrac{25}{AB}$

$AB = 93.3$

In $\triangle DBC$, $Tan\ D = \dfrac{BC}{DB}$

$Tan\ 35° = \dfrac{25}{DB}$

$DB = 35.7$

Distance between the ships $= AD = AB - DB$

$= 93.3 - 35.7 = 57.6\ m$

Video Suggestions

Please conduct a search on either YouTube or Teacher Tube to find appropriate videos for this lesson. Below are some suggested title searches:

➤ Geometry and Basic Trigonometry Ratios

➤ Solve Right Triangles – Part 2 Applications

➤ Law of Sines

➤ Law of Cosines

➤ Introduction to Vectors

Independent Instruction: Working On Your Own

Questions

☞ <u>Problem 1:</u> Solve the following oblique triangle?

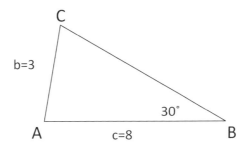

☞ <u>Problem 2:</u> A boy is flying a kite. At a height of 50 yards the angle of elevation from the foot of the boy to the kite is 25°. Find the length of the string the boy let off?

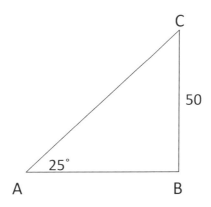

☞ <u>Problem 3:</u> Initial and terminal points of are (1, 2) and (3, –5), whereas, initial and terminal points of are (–2, 8) and (2, –6). Find if the vectors are equal, parallel or neither?

1. Using Sine Law,

    $$\frac{b}{Sin\,B} = \frac{c}{Sin\,C}$$

    $$\frac{3}{Sin\,30} = \frac{8}{Sin\,C}$$

    $$Sin\,C = \frac{8 \times Sin\,30}{3} = 1.33$$

    As, $Sin\,C > 1$, therefore, there exist no triangle with the dimensions given.

2. We need to find the length of the string i.e. AC.

    $$Sin\,A = \frac{BC}{AC}$$

    $$Sin\,25 = \frac{50}{AC}$$

    $$AC = \frac{50}{Sin\,25}$$

    $$AC = \frac{50}{0.4226} = 118.3$$

3. $\vec{u} = (3-1, -5-2) = (2, -7)$ $\quad$ *and* $\quad$ $\vec{v} = (2+2, -6-8) = (4, -14)$

    $$|\vec{u}| = \sqrt{(2)^2 + (-7)^2} = \sqrt{4+49} = \sqrt{53}$$

    $$|\vec{v}| = \sqrt{(4)^2 + (-14)^2} = \sqrt{16+196} = \sqrt{212}$$

    $$\textit{Direction of } \vec{u} = \tan^{-1}(\frac{y}{x}) = \tan^{-1}(\frac{-7}{2}) = -74.05°$$

    $$\textit{Direction of } \vec{v} = \tan^{-1}(\frac{y}{x}) = \tan^{-1}(\frac{-14}{4}) = -74.05°$$

    Magnitudes of vector u and v are not equal so they are not equal vectors, whereas, direction of both the vectors are same, therefore, vector u and v are parallel vectors.

Mini-Assessment

☞ **Problem 1:** If in an oblique triangle ABC, $a = 3$, $b = 4$ and $c = 5$. What will be the value of $\angle B$?

A. 90°

B. 55.13°

C. 53.13

D. 36.87°

E. 33.87°

☞ **Problem 2:** Two vectors are said to be parallel vectors if.

A. They have same magnitude.

B. They have same direction.

C. They have same magnitude and direction.

D. They have same magnitude and opposite direction.

E. They have same or opposite direction.

☞ **Problem 3:** The magnitude of a vector whose initial point is (1, −3) and terminal point is (−3, 5) is,

A. 8

B. $2\sqrt{2}$

C. $4\sqrt{5}$

D. 80

E. 2

☞ **Problem 4:** A 30 ft ladder is leaning against a building. If the foot of the ladder is 20 ft away from the wall, find the angle of elevation the ladder is making with the ground?

☞ **Problem 5:** A flying bird is making an angle of depression to the top of a 100m tall building is 25°. Find the altitude of the bird from the ground when its horizontal distance from the building is 70m?

☞ <u>**Problem 6:**</u> A pole is leaning 10° to the vertical. A man standing 30 yard away from the pole at the same side, the pole is leaning. Angle of elevation from the man's feet to the top of the pole is 33°. Find the height of the pole?

☞ <u>**Problem 7:**</u> Find the vector in component form, its magnitude and direction, if its initial and terminal points are (–5, –5) and (2, –8)?

Mini-Assessment Answers and Explanations

1. Option C.

2. Option E.

3. Option C.

4. We can make the following figure for this problem.

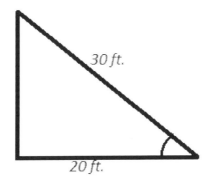

The angle of elevation for angle θ is:

$$\cos \theta = \frac{20}{30} \rightarrow \theta = \cos^{-1}\left(\frac{2}{3}\right) = 48.19°$$

5. We can make the following figure for this problem.

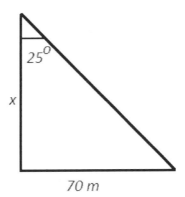

Altitude of the bird from the ground is:

$$\tan 25° = \frac{70}{x}$$

$$x = \frac{70}{\tan 25°} = 150.12 \text{ meters}$$

6. We can make the following figure for this situation:

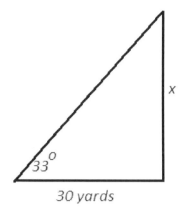

30 yards

The height of the pole is:

$\tan 33° = \frac{x}{30} \rightarrow x = 30 * \tan 33° = 19.48$ yards

7. The vector is:

$$A = \begin{pmatrix} 2 - (-5) \\ -8 - (-5) \end{pmatrix} = \begin{pmatrix} 7 \\ -3 \end{pmatrix} = 7i - 3j$$

The magnitude of the given vector is: $|A| = \sqrt{(7)^2 + (-3)^2} = \sqrt{58}$

The direction of the given vector is: $\hat{A} = \frac{\vec{A}}{|A|} = \frac{7i - 3j}{\sqrt{58}} = \frac{7}{\sqrt{58}}i - \frac{3}{\sqrt{58}}j$

Lesson Reflection

Angle of Elevation

If an object is above the observer, the angle made by the eye of the observer to the horizontal line in order to look up at the object is called the angle of elevation.

Angle of Depression

If an object is below the observer, the angle made by the eye of the observer to the horizontal line in order to look down at the object is called the angle of depression.

Laws of Sines

$$\frac{a}{Sin\,A} = \frac{b}{Sin\,B} = \frac{c}{Sin\,C}$$

Law of Sines is best to use when the following information is given.

(i) SAA

(ii) ASA

(iii) SSA

Laws of Cosines

$$a^2 = b^2 + c^2 - 2bc\,Cos\,A$$
$$b^2 = a^2 + c^2 - 2ac\,Cos\,B$$
$$c^2 = a^2 + b^2 - 2ab\,Cos\,C$$

Laws of Cosines are best to use when the following information is given.

(i) SAS

(ii) SSS

Magnitude of Vector

The magnitude of a vector shown in a coordinate plane can be calculated using distance formula.

Direction of Vector

Direction of a vector is calculated as

$$Tan^{-1}\left(\frac{y}{x}\right)$$

Made in the USA
Middletown, DE
02 May 2022